THIS JOURNAL BELONGS TO ...

Student:
_____

IF FOUND, PLEASE RETURN.

Parent or Guardian:
_____

Email:
_____

Phone:
_____

Everyday Student Journal to Success
A Creativity Journal with Bullets and Lines
PUBLISHED BY EARTHATONE ENTERPRISES

Cover Model: Celai West
Cover Photo by Katie Moffitt for Earthatone Enterprises and The Chatty Chick (dot) com
Cover Design, Layout, and Formatting by Eartha Watts Hicks
Earthatone name and logo is a trademark of Earthatone Enterprises.
Printed in the United States of America.

Note: While every effort has been made to ensure the accuracy of the information presented in this calendar, author/owner/publisher cannot be held liable for any errors, omissions, or inconsistencies.

Everyday Student Journal to Success

Everyday Student Journal to Success

Everyday Student Journal to Success

_____
_____
_____
_____
_____
_____
_____
_____
_____
_____
_____
_____
_____
_____
_____
_____
_____
_____
_____
_____
_____
_____
_____
_____
_____
_____
_____
_____
_____

Everyday Student Journal to Success

Everyday Student Journal to Success

Everyday Student Journal to Success

Everyday Student Journal to Success

Everyday Student Journal to Success

Everyday Student Journal to Success

Everyday Student Journal to Success

Everyday Student Journal to Success

Everyday Student Journal to Success

Everyday Student Journal to Success

_____

_____

_____

_____

_____

_____

_____

_____

_____

_____

_____

_____

_____

_____

_____

_____

_____

_____

_____

_____

_____

_____

_____

_____

_____

Everyday Student Journal to Success

Everyday Student Journal to Success

Everyday Student Journal to Success

Everyday Student Journal to Success

Everyday Student Journal to Success

Everyday Student Journal to Success

Everyday Student Journal to Success

Everyday Student Journal to Success

Everyday Student Journal to Success

Everyday Student Journal to Success

Everyday Student Journal to Success

Everyday Student Journal to Success

Everyday Student Journal to Success

Everyday Student Journal to Success

Everyday Student Journal to Success

Everyday Student Journal to Success

Everyday Student Journal to Success

Everyday Student Journal to Success

Everyday Student Journal to Success

_____
_____
_____
_____
_____
_____
_____
_____
_____
_____
_____
_____
_____
_____
_____
_____
_____
_____
_____
_____
_____
_____
_____
_____
_____
_____
_____
_____

Everyday Student Journal to Success

Everyday Student Journal to Success

Everyday Student Journal to Success

Everyday Student Journal to Success

Everyday Student Journal to Success

Everyday Student Journal to Success

Everyday Student Journal to Success

Everyday Student Journal to Success

Everyday Student Journal to Success

Everyday Student Journal to Success

Everyday Student Journal to Success

Everyday Student Journal to Success

Everyday Student Journal to Success

Everyday Student Journal to Success

Everyday Student Journal to Success

Everyday Student Journal to Success

#Celai
#CelaiWest
@CelaiWest

Facebook
Twitter
Instagram

Celai (suh-LAY) West

Celai West is a ten-year-old fashion model, known for her signature walk and especially for naturally styled hair on the runway. Her viral videos from runway footage and hair tutorials have generated 12 million+ views.

Celai has been modeling since the age of three and is now one of the choice child runway models for New York and Los Angeles Fashion Week, proudly sporting her natural hair. She's grateful knowing that others are encouraged by her example, hoping what she does can show other little girls that they are beautiful as they are. Celai also hopes to attend Howard University and become a designer.

A Lesson on Bullying....

Everyone has challenges to face, obstacles to overcome, and problems to resolve. While we all face our own unique circumstances, bullies prefer to make others feel unhappy or uncomfortable, which is unacceptable. And bullies usually continue to harass and torment others, because they get away with it. Bullies, even if they are children, can potentially be dangerous. In 2018, several instances of school violence have led to injuries and fatalities.

Your safety and well-being come first. Parents, teachers, and school counselors should *all* work together to ensure you thrive in a safe environment. Finding a solution, however, is not always simple. When matters are not easily resolved, parents must use their discretion to seek out the best viable options available under the circumstances.

If someone is teasing you, harassing you, taking your belongings without your permission, or threatening you with violence, there are ways to protect and defend yourself without getting into a physical altercation:

1. Notify your teacher and your parents as soon as possible.
2. Stay away from the bully.
3. If a bully is harassing you on social media, your parents should notify the guidance counselor and principal.
4. If at any time the matter escalates or becomes dangerous, your parents should seek police intervention, get a police report, and file for a restraining order. They should also consider a safety transfer.
5. If, at any time, you are attacked and seriously, physically injured, seek emergency room treatment, and get an aided police report right away .

October is National Bullying Prevention Month.

Be Strong Together is an organization that hopes to put an end to childhood bullying. Their site is a comprehensive online resource for parents and children in need. For more information, visit their website. (http://bstrongtogether.org/bullying/).

PACER's National Bullying Prevention Center provides innovative resources for students, parents, educators, and others, and recognizes bullying as a serious community issue that impacts education, physical and emotional health, and the safety and well-being of students. More information is available on their website. (http://www.pacer.org/bullying/getinvolved/partners/national.asp).

IDEAS

IDEAS

IDEAS

IDEAS

IDEAS

IDEAS

IDEAS

IDEAS

IDEAS

IDEAS

IDEAS

IDEAS

IDEAS

IDEAS

IDEAS

IDEAS

IDEAS

IDEAS

IDEAS

IDEAS

IDEAS

IDEAS

IDEAS

IDEAS

IDEAS

IDEAS

IDEAS

IDEAS

IDEAS

IDEAS

IDEAS

IDEAS

IDEAS

IDEAS

IDEAS

IDEAS

IDEAS

IDEAS

IDEAS

IDEAS

IDEAS

IDEAS

IDEAS

IDEAS

IDEAS

IDEAS

IDEAS

IDEAS

IDEAS

IDEAS

IDEAS

IDEAS

IDEAS

IDEAS

IDEAS

IDEAS

IDEAS

IDEAS

IDEAS

IDEAS

IDEAS

IDEAS

IDEAS

IDEAS

IDEAS

IDEAS

IDEAS

IDEAS

IDEAS

IDEAS

IDEAS

IDEAS

IDEAS

IDEAS

IDEAS

IDEAS

IDEAS

IDEAS

IDEAS

IDEAS

IDEAS

IDEAS

IDEAS

IDEAS

IDEAS

IDEAS

IDEAS

IDEAS

IDEAS

IDEAS

IDEAS

IDEAS

IDEAS

IDEAS

IDEAS

IDEAS

IDEAS

IDEAS

IDEAS

IDEAS

Address Book

Name:

Address:

Home Phone: Cell:

Facebook: Instagram:

Website: Other:

Name:

Address:

Home Phone: Cell:

Facebook: Instagram:

Website: Other:

Name:

Address:

Home Phone: Cell:

Facebook: Instagram:

Website: Other:

Name:

Address:

Home Phone: Cell:

Facebook: Instagram:

Website: Other:

Name:

Address:

Home Phone: Cell:

Facebook: Instagram:

Website: Other:

Name:

Address:

Home Phone: Cell:

Facebook: Instagram:

Website: Other:

Address Book

Name:

Address:

Home Phone: Cell:

Facebook: Instagram:

Website: Other:

Name:

Address:

Home Phone: Cell:

Facebook: Instagram:

Website: Other:

Name:

Address:

Home Phone: Cell:

Facebook: Instagram:

Website: Other:

Name:

Address:

Home Phone: Cell:

Facebook: Instagram:

Website: Other:

Name:

Address:

Home Phone: Cell:

Facebook: Instagram:

Website: Other:

Name:

Address:

Home Phone: Cell:

Facebook: Instagram:

Website: Other:

Address Book

Name:

Address:

Home Phone: Cell:

Facebook: Instagram:

Website: Other:

Name:

Address:

Home Phone: Cell:

Facebook: Instagram:

Website: Other:

Name:

Address:

Home Phone: Cell:

Facebook: Instagram:

Website: Other.

Name:

Address:

Home Phone: Cell:

Facebook: Instagram:

Website: Other:

Name:

Address:

Home Phone: Cell:

Facebook: Instagram:

Website: Other:

Name:

Address:

Home Phone: Cell:

Facebook: Instagram:

Website: Other:

Contents

Use the **Contents** pages to notate page numbers of any information you'd want to access quickly.

Page #		Subject
111	SAMPLE	IMPORTANT DETAILS ABOUT PLACEMENT TEST
180	SAMPLE	AFTER-SCHOOL PROGRAM OFFICE NUMBER

Contents

Page #	Subject

Made in the USA
Middletown, DE
19 August 2021